SCHOOL OF
Oud

MB21910

By Mavrothi Kontanis

 **FREE** Free Audio Online!
Visit: www.MelBay.com/21910

GW00567480

INTRODUCTION

The oud is a very special instrument with a long, rich history and an enduring legacy. The oud, also known as *ud*, *aoud*, and *outi,* is related to the Persian instrument known as the *barbat*, and both are likely descendants of an ancient lute–like instrument first seen during the Bronze Age in Mesopotamia. An early, four–course version of the oud was used by Arab–speaking peoples in the same region around 1,500 years ago, while the ouds we play today have been heavily influenced by several turn of the 20th century luthiers such as Emmanuel Venios (Manol) and the famed Nahat family, among others. Some important players we should all be familiar with include Nevres Bey, Yorgos Batzanos, Hrant Kenkulian, Şerif Muhiddin Targan, Çinucen Tanrikorur, Mohamad El Qasabji, Riad El Sunbati, Farid El Atrache, Jameel Bashir and George Michel, to name just a few.

The history of the oud and those who have cultivated it is truly impressive, but the real testament to its importance is that it is still so prevalent today. From traditional folk and classical music, to every possible combination of style and genre, the oud has taken on a global identity that continues to evolve.

An instrument which lies within so many different folk and classical musical traditions does pose a few challenges for students living in different parts of the world. In many cases, teachers are not easy to find, or perhaps complimentary resources are needed to enhance a student's lessons. In either case, this book and its accompanying CD attempt to present the basic groundwork needed to successfully study the oud and form the basis for continued study and improvement for the future. As you will see, the primary focus of this book is the study of *Makam* (Near Eastern musical modes) in the Ottoman tradition, specifically the makams *Rast*, *Mahur* and *Nikriz*. Using exercises, etudes and traditional repertoire, you will learn not only about these three beautiful makams, but also how to go about the study of makam in general.

No book or manual can magically make someone a good player, but every student does need guidance and encouragement to go hand in hand with their own personal effort. Many things need to be coordinated at once, both physically and mentally, and this can sometimes prove to be a bit intimidating. The best approach when feeling discouraged is to identify the problem, and then simplify it until it has been mastered. For example, if there is a difficult passage with 20 notes, it should be slowed down and dissected into smaller parts; taking five notes, or even two at a time, until each piece is easily combined with the others. This applies to ideas as well. Some conventions in Near Eastern music can seem complicated at first, and the notation we use is imperfect and sometimes confusing. However, if you take things a few steps at a time, with patience and regular review, you will see that everything will fall into place. Remember that sheet music only serves as a guide, and that the true work and art come through your musical interpretation of any given piece. Use the recordings on the accompanying CD to help you get started, and continue to explore the wealth of recordings that exist not just for your enjoyment, but for your education as well.

The oud, like any musical instrument, requires love and hard work. Patience, repetition and creativity are key to a meaningful study. When practicing a piece, understand that each note of each passage is important, containing its own story and identity, just as each player has a story and identity of their own. Listen carefully, and root yourself in the tradition, while never losing sight of who you are as an individual. Let what you have learned enhance your own voice and enrich it, not control it. In the end, music is simply about communicating to your audience as truthfully and effectively as possible.

So be sure to listen, and then let yourself be heard.

Mavrothi T. Kontanis

For additional tips and information on the oud and the music theory related to it, feel free to use the following website as a general resource: www.oudcafe.com.

Many thanks to Dr. Eric Ederer for his feedback and guidance regarding the introductory pages of this book.

OUD FUNDAMENTALS

For good, comfortable posture, follow these basic guidelines:

Keep your back straight and your shoulders even. Rest the oud on your thigh, on the side of your picking hand, with the face of the oud perpendicular to the ground or leaning slightly forward. The oud should stay comfortably in place supported between the forearm of your picking hand, your thigh and your abdomen. Angle the neck out from your body slightly to form a triangle between the bowl of the oud, your left shoulder (if you are right–handed) and the pegbox.

Most players use a foot stool to raise the leg supporting the oud to a comfortable height. Your wrist will be slightly bent, but make sure to keep your hands relaxed so you can enjoy many hours of playing without any discomfort.

Tips regarding your oud pick:

Your pick, also called *mizrap* or *risha*, can be made of various materials, including plastic, animal horn, tortoise shell, or even eagle feather. Since some of these materials are rare and protected, most players use plastic or horn of varying thickness and flexibility. Experiment with making picks on your own or modifying mass produced picks to see what works best for you.

Balance your pick in your hand so that it lines up along the crease where your fingers meet your palm. Stabilize it between your thumb, first and fourth fingers for even pressure. Keep your hands relaxed, using mostly wrist motions for picking and strumming, and arch the fingers of your other hand to cleanly hit your notes with the tips of your fingers.

There are two basic types of picking strokes: *rest strokes* and *free strokes*. A rest stroke is made by resting the pick on the string below after sounding your target note, as part of your follow through. Free strokes, on the other hand, do not come in contact with adjacent strings, and your follow through arches slightly outward, away from the oud. In general, use rest strokes for down strokes, and always use free strokes for up strokes.

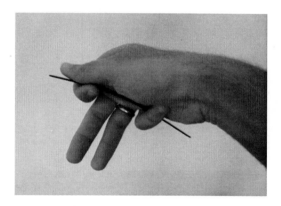 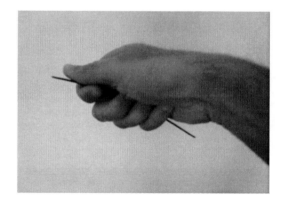

Tunings for the oud:

Many tunings are used for the oud, most of which have 6 courses (5 double strings and 1 single string). Some common ones are listed here in concert pitch. The first group of tunings will work best with this book and its accompanying CD, however you can tune your oud in any way you wish, as long as you take any difference into account when playing along with the CD. Always be sure the tuning you use is compatible with your oud. Tunings are listed with the lowest note to the left progressing to the most treble note on the right. The top grouping belongs to what are known as "Turkish" ouds, with the tuning in bold indicating the tuning used for this book. The bottom grouping is for Arabic ouds, the last of which is used on an Iraqi oud with 6 courses.

E A B e a d' I D A B e a d' I C# F# B e a d' I B F# B e a d' I D F# B e a d' I E F# B e a d'

C F A d g c' I D G A d g c' I C E A d g c' I F A d g c' f' I F C D g c' f'

3

OTTOMAN MUSIC

Ottoman music refers to the blend of urban, folk and court music of the Ottoman Empire, which for several centuries controlled most of the Eastern Mediterranean and Near East. With its center in cosmopolitan Istanbul (Constantinople), the music reflects the influences of the many diverse ethnic and religious groups of the region over the course of time, including some Western musical influences as well.

In the early 20th century, the Ottoman Empire ceased to exist, yet the music continued on, mostly in Turkey, and took on the name *Türk Sanat Musikisi*. It is around this time that we see a strong break between Arabic and Ottoman music. In the Arab countries, for the most part, fixed tones are used to define the intervals of a given makam (musical mode), including whole tones, half tones, and quarter tones, though in practice intonation can vary. Typically in Western music, there are only whole and half tones, which generally defines *tempered* music. In Ottoman music, we see more possibilities, including 9 subdivisions within each whole step and 4 subdivisions in each half step. These subdivisions are called *komas*, and when playing non–tempered notes, or *microtones*, we often hear slight shifts in pitch in these notes as we pass over them in a melody. When ascending, often the pitch of the microtone is played slightly higher. When descending, the microtonal note can be played slightly lower. These details add depth to both the playing and listening experience, and accentuate the sense of movement in a melody.

Earlier in history, Ottoman music was notated using a system similar to Byzantine notation, known as *Hamparsoom Nota*. Today, a modified version of Western notation is used, though as mentioned in the introduction, it is not perfect. Certain things have to be understood when it comes to Ottoman notation, and more will be said on this later. Those shortcomings aside, we naturally come to the conclusion that if there are more notes being used than in Western tempered music, we need more accidentals (sharps and flats) to describe on paper which notes are to be played. The accidentals used in Ottoman music are listed below, and you will see that only intervals of 1, 4, 5, 8, 9 and 12 koma(s) are specified, along with a letter symbolizing the number of komas in the interval.

	1 Koma = F	4 Komas = B	5 Komas = S	8 Komas = K	9 Komas = T	12 Komas = A
Sharp	‡	♯	♯	♯	𝄪	(no accidental)
Flat	◁	♭	♭	♭	𝄫	(no accidental)

Please note that the 4 koma sharp (♯) is played slightly flatter than the Western, tempered sharp. The 5 koma sharp (♯) is slightly higher than the tempered sharp.

So, what is a makam? Is it some kind of scale?

A makam is much more than just a scale. Several makams may contain the same basic scale while remaining very different from each other.

We can think of a makam as a partially written song, complete with basic scale(s), melodic progression (*Seyir*) and characteristic phrases. These elements guide us in composing both a set piece or an improvisation (*Taksim*), while still allowing us to create a very unique piece of music. Why bother using a makam that may be hundreds of years old or more? For the same reasons we don't reinvent a language, words, catch phrases or gestures each time we try to communicate to someone. What some might call "rules" of a makam are actually built-in tools and pathways that make it easier to express thoughts and emotions through the music. Makams aid us in effectively tapping into our own humanity, and inspire us to greater heights of creativity. As you study the makams introduced in this book, my hope is that it will not only reinforce your love of the oud and of the selected music, but will also lead you to explore more repertoire, more makams, and inspire you to compose pieces of your own in the makams that speak most to you.

There are three general makam categories for seyir:

Ascending: Begins in the Tonic range, then shows us the Dominant and Upper Octave ranges, in that order, before resolving back to the Tonic.

Descending: Begins in the Upper Octave range, works its way down to the Tonic via the Dominant, then jumps up again, reaching even higher, before concluding with a path through the Dominant to the Tonic.

Ascending–Descending: Begins in the middle (Dominant) range, then continues to develop before concluding with a path through the Dominant to the Tonic.

THEORY BASICS

Tetrachords and pentachords

The basic scale of a makam consists of a tetrachord and pentachord combined. Here are some examples:

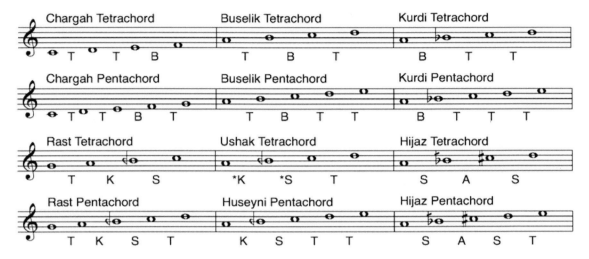

* In practice the makam Ushak has the K and S intervals reversed, though the accidentals are kept the same in the notation.

In Ottoman music, pieces are generally written in the keys of G (SOL) or A (LA). This is done for ease in defining the specific intervals between each note. The player reading the music may perform the piece in any key they wish. This can be a challenge in the beginning, but like most things, is just a matter of practice and familiarity. For the purposes of this book and the accompanying CD, all notes are transposed down a fourth, meaning that G = D (SOL = RE), A = E (LA = MI), B = F# (SI = FA#), C = G (DO = SOL), D = A (RE = LA), E = B (MI = SI), F = C (FA = DO), etc.

Names of the notes

Examples of note names in Ottoman music:

In Ottoman music, we see that each individual note has a name. Over time you will realize that these names are not random, but are related to makams in which a given note stands out in one way or another, whether it is a tonic, dominant, or some other prominent note in a makam. Remember, regardless of what key you are playing in, these note names remain constant as fixed place holders in the scale of the makam. For example, the tonic of Rast makam will always be the note *rast* , and the fifth of Rast makam will always be the note *neva*, etc, whatever key you decide use.

GENERAL EXERCISES

Exercises 1 and 2 focus on the left hand. Play each measure in Ex. 1 for at least 1-3 minutes to build strength in the left hand. Repeat melody patterns in Ex. 2 on all the strings using a basic minor scale to help acquaint you with the notes throughout the entire fingerboard. Remember that in the recordings you will hear these notes a fourth down from where they are written in the score. Also remember that when playing a melody on only one string, we use alternate picking starting with a down stroke, picking: down up, down up…

Exercise 1 [Track 1]: Try to keep your lower fingers planted as you play through the exercise.

Exercise 2 [Track 2]: Use suggested fingerings to play entire exercise on one string.

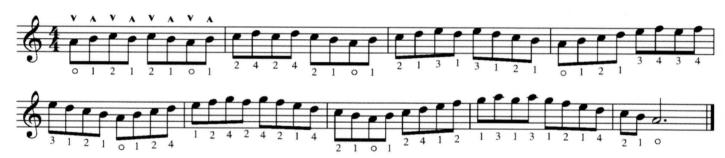

Exercise 3 focuses on the right and left hands using the G (SOL) major scale, played for you in D (RE) on Track 3 of the accompanying CD. Down strokes with the pick should generally be rest strokes for optimal volume and quality of tone, while up strokes should be free strokes. Typically on the oud we play across the strings like we are playing triplets, with a down stroke each time we change strings, picking: down up down, down up down… When we are playing only on one string again, our picking pattern is: down up, down up…

Exercise 3 [Track 3]: Pay close attention to string numbers, fingerings and picking direction for this exercise.

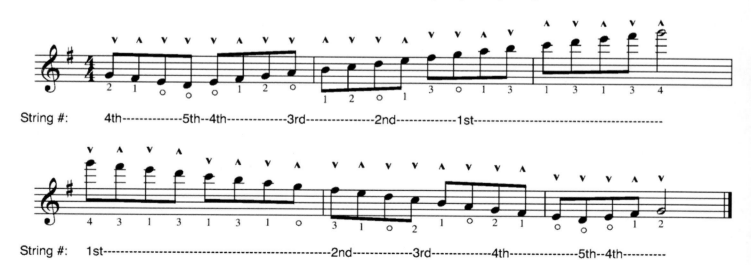

MAKAM RAST

Scale diagram

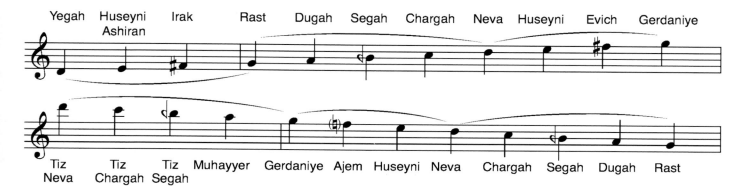

Rast is a very beautiful ascending makam, with a basic scale resembling a major scale with slightly flat third and seventh degrees. Rast typically moves from the region of the lower tonic to the fifth, returning to the tonic, and rising to the upper octave before resolving again on the lower tonic. In addition to these main focal notes, pieces in Rast also often stress the second, third and fourth degrees of the scale, with important cadences between the second and fifth. Throughout this makam's melodic development, certain notes such as the seventh and fourth degrees are often adjusted according to the direction of the melody. You will also see that many makam modulations are possible, some of the most common being: *Segah, Suzinak* and *Nikriz*.

Modulation examples

- Segah makam elements, see measure #'s 56-59 in the Rast Peshrev
- Suzinak makam elements, see measure #'s 34-42 in the Rast Peshrev
- Nikriz makam elements, see measure #'s 80-81 in the Rast Peshrev

Pay attention to the intonation of the notes in the pieces using the recordings to guide you, and feel free to add your own ornamentation style to them over time. There is a wealth of recordings and written scores available in this makam, so take advantage of that and immerse yourself in the music as much as you can.

Rast Exercise [Track 4]

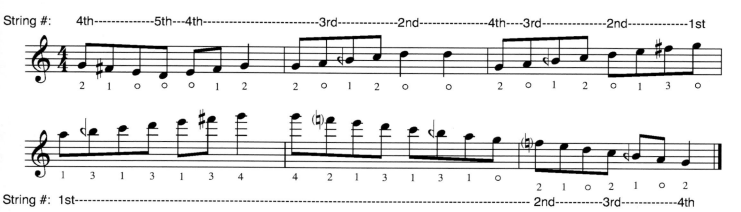

Additional Rast track listings

- **Rast Etude #1 [Track 5]**
- **Rast Etude #2 [Track 6]**
- **Rast Sirto [Track 7]**
- **Rast Peshrev [Track 8]**
- **Rast Saz Semai [Track 9]**

Rast Etude #1

Rhythm: Nim Sofyan

M. T. Kontanis

♩ = 92

Rast Etude #2

Rhythm: Aksak

♪ = 220

M. T. Kontanis

Rast Sirto

Traditional
Arranged by M. T. Kontanis

Rhythm: Nim Sofyan

♩= 60

Rast Peshrev

Rhythm: Duyek

♪=138

Kemani Tatyos Efendi

Arranged by M. T. Kontanis

Rast Saz Semai

Kemani Tatyos Efendi
Arranged by M. T. Kontanis

Rhythm: Aksak Semai
♪ = 112

MAKAM MAHUR

Scale diagram

Tiz   Tiz   Tiz
Neva Chargah Buselik Muhayyer Gerdaniye Mahur Huseyni Neva Chargah Buselik Dugah Rast Gevesht

Tiz Muhayyer Gerdaniye Mahur Huseyni Neva Evich Huseyni Neva Gerdaniye Ajem Huseyni Neva
Buselik

Mahur is a classic descending makam, with a basic scale resembling a major scale. Mahur typically moves from the region of the upper tonic briefly to the sixth, then to the fifth, then rising to the upper octave before terminating on the lower tonic. Mahur rarely travels to the lower fifth, often stressing the lower sixth instead. Additionally, the second, third, fourth and seventh are often stressed in unique ways which you will see in the repertoire. As noted in Rast, certain notes such as the third, fourth and seventh degrees are often adjusted according to the direction of the melody, and many makam modulations are possible, some of the most common being: *Rast, Segah* and *Nikriz*.

Modulation examples

- Rast makam elements, see measure # 5 in the Mahur Saz Semai
- Segah makam elements, see measure #'s 9-10 in the Mahur Saz Semai
- Nikriz makam elements, see measure #'s 15-18 in the Mahur Zeybek

Pay attention to the intonation of the notes in the pieces using the recordings to guide you, and feel free to add your own ornamentation style to them over time. There is a wealth of recordings and written scores available in this makam, so take advantage of that and immerse yourself in the music as much as you can.

Mahur Exercise [Track 10]

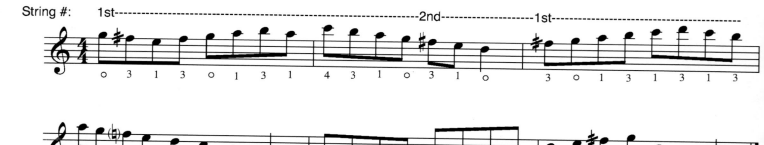

Additional Mahur track listings

- **Mahur Etude #1 [Track 11]**
- **Mahur Etude #2 [Track 12]**
- **Mahur Zeybek [Track 13]**
- **Mahur Peshrev [Track 14]**
- **Mahur Saz Semai [Track 15]**

16

Mahur Etude #1

Rhythm: Yuruk Semai

♩ = 104

M. T. Kontanis

Mahur Etude #2

Rhythm: Jurjuna

M. T. Kontanis

♪ = 200

Mahur Zeybek

Rhythm: Aksak

♩ = 108

Traditional
Arranged by M. T. Kontanis

19

Mahur Peshrev

Rhythm: Duyek
♪ = 116

Gazi Giray Han
Arranged by M. T. Kontanis

Mahur Saz Semai

Rhythm: Aksak Semai
♪ = 108

Nikolakis
Arranged by M. T. Kontanis

MAKAM NIKRIZ

Scale diagram

Nikriz is ascending—descending, taking the basic scale of *Hijaz* makam, but with the tonic one step lower on the note rast, giving this makam a minor flavor. Nikriz begins with a focus around the fifth and then moves between the upper octave and tonic before coming to rest on the tonic. In addition to these main focal points, pieces in Nikriz also stress the second, third and seventh degrees of the scale, as well as the lower fifth. Throughout this makam's melodic development the seventh degree is often adjusted according to the direction of the melody. Nikriz makam is used in many old folk songs from the Aegean Sea region, and pieces in Nikriz are often full of makam modulations, some of the most common being: *Rast*, *Segah* and *Evich*.

Modulation examples

- Rast makam elements, see measure # 12 in the Nikriz Saz Semai
- Segah makam elements, see measure # 9 in the Nikriz Saz Semai
- Evich makam elements, see measure # 7 in the Nikriz Saz Semai

The last piece in this lesson, the Nikriz Saz Semai by the composer Refik Fersan, is by the far the most challenging piece covered in this book. Take your time with it, and try to listen to the wonderful recording of Udi Yorgos Batzanos and orchestra performing this incredible Saz Semai for added inspiration.

Nikriz Exercise [Track 16]

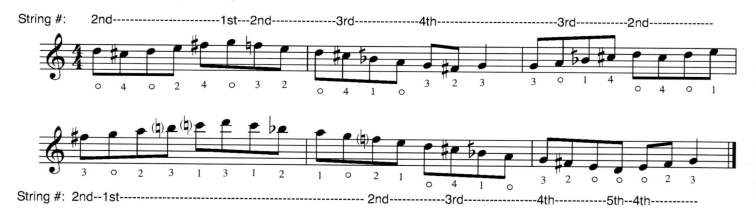

Additional Nikriz track listings

- **Nikriz Etude #1 [Track 17]**
- **Nikriz Etude #2 [Track 18]**
- **Nikriz Longa #1 [Track 19]**
- **Nikriz Longa #2 [Track 20]**
- **Nikriz Saz Semai [Track 21]**

Nikriz Etude #1

Rhythm: Devri Hindi

♪ = 208

M. T. Kontanis

Nikriz Etude #2

Rhythm: Sofyan

M. T. Kontanis

♩ = 92

26

Nikriz Longa #1

Rhythm: Nim Sofyan

♩ = 112

Tanburi Jemil Bey
Arranged by M. T. Kontanis

27

Nikriz Longa #2

Rhythm: Nim Sofyan

♩ = 94

Tanburi Jemil Bey
Arranged by M. T. Kontanis

Nikriz Saz Semai

Rhythm: Aksak Semai
♪ = 108

Refik Fersan
Arranged by M. T. Kontanis

29

Rhythms

Nim Sofyan [Track 22]

Aksak (Karshilama) [Track 23]

Duyek [Track 24]

Aksak Semai [Track 25]

Yuruk Semai [Track 26]

Jurjuna [Track 27]

Aksak (Zeybek) [Track 28]

Devri Hindi [Track 29]

Sofyan [Track 30]